STOP

HOMELESSNESS...FOREVER!

A PRACTICAL GUIDE WITH TIPS AND SECRETS FOR

VOLUNTEERS-ORGANIZATIONS-GOVERNMENT + YOU

TO HELP AND SHOW

HOMELESS MEN OR WOMEN (WITH OR WITHOUT KIDS)

HOW TO

END THE MISERY OF BEING HOMELESS!

By Herbert C. Anderson Jr., M.S. (60 years' experience)

LARGE PRINT

This Large Print edition's text is unabridged. Set in 16 pt.

Published by JH Enterprises LLC, Socorro, NM in the United States of America.

Printed in the United States of America.

Library of Congress Cataloging in Publication Data, LCCN: 2015920001

ISBN-13:978-1519577474
ISBN-10:1519577478

NONFICTION BOOKS
BY
HERBERT C. ANDERSON JR., M.S.

The Life, The Times and The Art
Of
Branson Graves Stevenson

And

A Computerized
Poison Information Retrieval System

DEDICATION

This book is dedicated to my Mother, Vena V. Anderson, and Father, Herbert C. Anderson Sr., who taught me very early in life to help the homeless, the poor and those whom tragedy visited plus the first Mission for homeless men in which I volunteered at the age of 18.

APPRECIATION

I appreciate the efforts and proofreading endeavors of these who labored thusly:

C. Bonner Oates, D.D.S.

Orban W. Winton, Jr., B.S.

Laurie J. Chan, M.A.

Thank you all for your fine work and patience!

Sincerely,

Herbert C. Anderson Jr. M.S.
Author

PREFACE

The purpose of this practical guide is to give the reader:

- An overview with some depth of what it means to be "homeless",
- Some reasons why people become homeless,
- Illustrations of usual methods to help homeless men and women currently in use throughout most of the country,
- As well as show what will really help those of the homeless population who wish to return to the community of their choice and its society as positive assets, e.g., as productive members who can support themselves.

Further, this guide will provide suggestions of how you personally can use your time as a volunteer or a paid member of a staff fulfilling the mission you work with.

For those of you who are in Think Tanks or on committees offering suggestions to your community regarding more efficient or practical ways of changing or continuing current services to aid the homeless men and women in your locality to better their lives is the reason this guide offers various suggestions.

Every suggestion in this guide works to stop homelessness and is a method I used over my some sixty years of working with homeless men, women and women with a child or children.

Instead of using the motel example illustrated In the last chapter I used an alternate method, the hotel floor shown on page 95.

Reader, your ideas and time are important as an individual or a staff member of an organization, church, non-profit, business, government or other entity in the betterment of services to the homeless persons of your locale.

TABLE OF CONTENTS

Understanding Homeless People
and Their Needs: Page   9

Shelter Availability and
Other Assistance: Page 21

Census: Page 33

Past Similarities: Page 44

Volunteering Suggestions: Page 52

Ideas to Help Homeless People
Win: Page 89

Stimulating Compassion: Page 102

Suggestions: Page 122

Most of Our Ideas to Help
Homeless People Need Change: Page 127

How to End Homelessness: Page 133

Honors: Page 163

Understanding Homeless People
And
Their Needs

The word "HOMELESS" stimulates all sorts of images in our minds of what and who a homeless person is...and most of it is wrong!

Yet when we give to charities and organizations which advertise that our money and volunteer time "takes care of the homeless", we feel wonderful that we've helped the "poor homeless".

Granted, we should feel good about that donation of our money and time because it does some good.

Yet, mostly what it does is help some homeless persons for a moment in time.

Really, what it does is lock them forever into a wretched, miserable, no hope environment called "homeless".

Why?

Because all those homeless persons do is recycle day after day and never or only rarely return to the community with respect and independency.

For example, one meal perhaps three times a week is certainly about the limit of the money often available to feed local homeless men and women (with or without children) that an organization, church, non-profit or other entity has a budget for or can do.

However, you and I eat 20 to 21 meals each week...and they eat from the soup line about 3 meals each week.

As good as those meals given to the homeless men and women, with or without children, are for one hour of filling the tummy inside and warm if there is a place to eat inside...and outside in the cold if there's no warm inside sitting.

The reality is that the rest of the food/meals have to be found by:

- begging for money (panhandling),
- searching the garbage cans for food,
- obtain a few non-perishable cans of food from the local food storehouse,

- stop by a church for can food once or twice a month, sometimes once a week,
- hopefully find or borrow a can opener,
- maybe find a kind person who'll buy a sandwich or hamburger meal,

so with this combination of possibilities, if most of them produce some results, then perhaps the homeless person can eat maybe 40% to 60% of the 21 meals most of the rest of us eat.

Who can study for a job or learn a skill when most of their time is used to hunt food or perhaps eating is reduced to one meal a day or every couple of days?

Can you? Can I?

NO!

The point is...YES, homeless folks devour food given to them. Yet, what is there for them after they've had their fill at the moment?

Are they helped to change their life

and find independency to support themselves in the community?

What about jobs and/or education or some other gainful existence are they helped to perform, so they can stop being homeless and earn a living plus eating regular meals on their own money?

NO!

The homeless people are helped to stay homeless by irregular eating and inconsistent shelter and additional problems or concerns we'll discuss.

They are shown no direction for learning how to stop being homeless and support themselves...many had places in the community like you and I prior to becoming homeless...and they miss it!

Yet, for the moment, we need to continue to support those organizations and governments who help the homeless in some way until we find a better solution.

Hungry people will keep what they can...hidden in a cache or in their clothes or gorge themselves when food is available regardless of the health consequences.

Attention to the food health triangle of vegetables, fruit, meat, fish and other daily recommendations, as well as properly cooked food temperatures usually aren't followed unless a food line or soup kitchen is serving.

This is because homeless individuals don't have any way to:
- cook a meal or
- place to eat it or
- often the utensils to use in eating or
- somewhere to wash up.

Churches and other organizations may serve a wholesome meal once or twice or more a week and those who eat do appreciate the service.

Shelters may serve a supper meal, however only those admitted to the shelter are permitted to eat. This may be the only meal served per day.

A few cities fund one or more organizations to serve one to three meals daily for anyone who stands in line. Hundreds in larger cities are served.

A majority are probably homeless people. No one knows who is homeless and who is not, unless the organization serving surveys those in line.

It is difficult to mention it, however some homeless frequent unlocked garbage areas of grocery stores, restaurants and similar firms for food at night.

Stay in a shelter, if a city has shelters, is usually a night or two with an occasional shelter allowing either a week or two, then homeless men or women or women with children are discharged into any kind of weather after their shelter time expires.

If these individuals are in a program or project to help them stop being homeless, expulsion from a shelter disrupts their progress toward ending their homelessness drastically.

Discharge for any of these homeless is basically the same for most shelter termination times because the shelter funding usually specifies how long a person can stay in a shelter.

Length of stay in a shelter is so designated to insure that the shelter stay is available to all who seek shelter over a period of time.

Consistent shelter is important to the success of helping a homeless person to stop being homeless and complete the program/project for ending his/her homelessness.

Without continuous safe shelter, a place to wash up, and shower, it is almost impossible for a homeless person to stop being homeless.

In cities which have parks with trees, homeless individuals and families sleep at night.

Kids are tied on the upper branches and the rest of the family sleeps elsewhere in the same or a nearby tree until daybreak, then they all leave the trees and go to the streets before the park rangers or police patrol the area.

Homeless persons find places:

- out of the way of traffic to sleep at night,
- sometimes in a group for protection from the local bullies, rascals and thugs of the area because
- both the groups and single persons sleeping need to be alert to the danger of being beaten, mugged, raped and robbed during the night.

Some are killed.

Often, many of the homeless are

military veterans who fought bravely, were wounded and now are on the streets, sleeping under bridges and living in the worst squalor because there is no other way of living.

Some survive long enough to regain society, however most die unknown in unmarked passing, occasionally found stone cold.

It is the same fate which death reserves for other homeless who are the unloved, forgotten men, women, and women with children.

Not helping homeless people to a better fate or where possible to come back into the community with education and/or employment or some manner of supporting themselves is our national shame!

Our country…yes, it needs to help other countries, however we need to learn to help our people first and we're doing poorly at that and have been for decades and more than a century.

So, it is necessary to learn how to help homeless stop being homeless.

And, hopefully with this practical guide the reader will be better equipped to provide aid to the homeless people in a knowledgeable way, as well as over time create better ways to extinguishing the homeless environment as much as possible.

It is time to stop keeping homeless men, women, and women with children in our country in this hopeless environment of misery.

We need to develop effective methods to help these persons return to society and the community with dignity, independence and respect.

Yet for now, it is necessary that we continue our present way of helping these people until methods in various communities are better developed and solutions are created and funded.

Helping homeless men, women, and women with children to stop being homeless can be done by using a coordinated effort for all of us in a community, village, city, rural area or other environment to work together to provide effective services, perhaps with a joint partnership toward a decided goal.

Some communities are doing or considering taking a homeless census in their community to learn the depth of the homeless population in their urban city or rural town or village.

Such a census may be useful in determining how much help will be required to assist the homeless population...and it may shock the senses of each citizen of the locality enough for them to do something.

This guide will offer suggestions by helping you determine what you can do with what you have to stop homelessness by yourself and/or working with various organizations and people.

Over time this will start giving hope to homeless men, women, and women with children for tomorrow while taking care of their current daily needs.

It will also encourage them mentally and physically to return to society and eventually cease their years of wandering and recycling so currently prevalent in urban and rural America or your locale.

SHELTER AVAILABILITY
AND
OTHER ASSISTANCE

Homeless men, women and women with children are not all addicts, drunks and lazy people. They are not trash either!

These are persons who need our help and for the most part of my over sixty years of working with them, the majority want to return to the community and its society where a great majority used to live...perhaps some were your neighbors.

It is hard to live:

- on the street,
- under bridges,
- on tree branches,
- sleep in a door way,
- be a homeless who can be arrested in some cities for being a vagrant, getting a misdemeanor police record

…and not be distressed!

Living in a shelter funded by the city or town or church or other entity is no picnic, either.

Yet, living on the street using cardboard pieces or boxes for cover at night to keep out the cold is downright dangerous and deprives one of a good night's rest because the person sleeping needs to be alert for danger.

It may be necessary to fight to stay alive or keep what little possessions a person has because local bullies or thugs, usually in gangs, attack homeless people wherever they find them.

Attacks usually happen if the attackers think they can overpower the male homeless individual when he sleeps alone.

In these episodes homeless women or women with children are treated worse by being raped and/or beaten, disappear from the streets or return to the streets, some finding the way to a hospital and others simply pass away. The children are often orphaned.

Cities of 800,000 and above often have a homeless population of 8,000 or more and many cities learn the number of homeless persons is greater when a census is taken.

Some cities conduct a census annually which gives sort of an idea of their homeless populations existing in their localities in a shelter(s), as well as outside of a shelter(s).

It is good practice for rural areas and smaller cities or town to learn really how many and what kind of homeless people they have, i.e., whether the homeless persons are men or women or women with children and any other pertinent information about them in order to provide proper assistance.

Some rural areas have homeless who are turned out by their families and relatives in the spring, summer and fall months, then allow them back during the winter months. This practice appears to be common in rural areas and less in larger cities.

Apparently, cities of 800,000 population average about 8,000 or more homeless persons and offer shelter beds available to be about 1400 beds on any given night. This means about one person has a shelter bed and 5 or 6 homeless individuals find there is no room or bed for them each night.

Allowance to stay in a shelter can vary from one night to about 14 nights.

When one enters most shelters, whatever is carried in, including clothes, knives, books, trash and other possessions is checked in, put in a bulk bag and stored by shelter monitors.

The persons being sheltered for the night are given pajamas and required to shower and sleep in the clean pajamas. Pajamas are returned in the morning in exchange for the belongings checked the night before. Clean pajamas are given each night.

Very few shelters provide either breakfast or an evening meal. It is rare the homeless person can stay in a shelter during the day.

So whatever the weather...snow, rain, cold, windy, nice...that's what the homeless person, with or without kids, is exposed to during the day while looking for a meal and to somehow stay warm or cool and safe.

When the homeless individual, with or without children needs to leave the shelter because his or her time of being there is over, they go out in whatever weather conditions confront them.

Some Missions have a day room

where men, women and women with children can sit from mid-morning to around 4 p.m. which, as long as there is room, the public is welcome to use and these Missions are men's night shelters.

The many who use the Day Room won't be included in the shelter stay for that evening, since the shelter is for men only.   The   day   room   is   constantly monitored.

Homeless   people   are   generally looked at as a blight on the city or town because they loiter often in tourist areas, sleep in business doorways, beg for money everywhere on the streets, including   the   business   districts   and target anywhere someone will visit or congregate.

Showers for the homeless usually are   available   in   only   shelters. Occasionally,   an   organization   will provide weekly free showers.   Even then, with infrequent showers or other bathing facilities results in the homeless emitting a disagreeable odor to some people.

Yet, readers please remember the homeless are still people who may once have been your neighbors, maybe even a relative.

Homeless people don't have anything to help them return to society and/or the community...unless ways are found to assist them back to these environments, giving them hope, a work training education and other assistance.

Over the years, I've observed that most homeless want to contribute to the community and stop being homeless.

Granted, shelters are helpful to a point. Certainly two weeks of relief with a safe bed, food, bath facilities and clean clothes increase one's attitude positively. Sure, a shelter is useful even if that is all it does.

However, if that's it, i.e., all it does…the shelter is just a temporary relief which doesn't do much to solve the plight of the homeless…nor does it really give any solutions to the village, city or township to eliminate homelessness because these people have nowhere to go when they leave the shelter.

There are exceptions.

For example, occasionally I've placed a homeless man into a commercial truck school of intensive learning which in a week to ten days the person graduated as a commercial truck driver with licensing when funding for the school was available.

All genders of homeless people who came to me for help over the years, as well as when I worked during the day for non-profit organizations or volunteered on the street at night or worked the ghettos, mostly wanted to work and escape homelessness.

Reducing homelessness and creating a pathway to return to the community using education and employment of previously homeless people ensures the future of the city, township, and/or village.

Programs for homeless conversion to more constructive living need to be seven days a week activities with rest over enough weeks to equip the homeless individual to manage his/her life once they leave the project.

Organizations with limited budgets, yet sufficient to perhaps provide a meal once or twice or three times weekly or more still should continue to do so. Those homeless people outside a program to end homelessness still should be helped until they can get into a homelessness elimination project.

Most communities recognize the value in providing some relief to the homeless, even though it may be insufficient to solve the homeless person's need and return to self-sufficiency.

Medical and eye exams are important additional services when starting a program to assist homeless people. The diagnosis may be helpful for the case manager or mentor in providing education and/or employment.

There are other services which will be discussed later in this guide book.

Some homeless persons have mental issues and can't be helped by the usual average rehabilitation programs, yet they need help. Years ago, there were "group homes" which assisted these people and those homes were funded principally by some government department(s) and apparently some other entities such as grant funding.

However when that funding ceased and the group homes were discontinued, then the people in them were mostly released to the street, apparently.

It appears people of this ilk wander the street throughout the country hopelessly and aimlessly for the most part. People of this nature usually may not fit in a standard homeless persons' program with the goal of termination of homelessness, so helping them may require a separate program.

This Practical Guide is a detailed collection of effective, time tested, suggestions this author used, experienced and/or observed over sixty years of helping homeless men, women and women with children to be self-reliant and by showing them tools and ways to return to the community as productive contributing individuals.

Also, it will provide examples of who the homeless are, how to help those wishing to leave the environment of homelessness and return to the community with independence and employment and/or education to sustain them to continue live away from being homeless and its subsequent misery.

Reader, the difference between you and me and a homeless person is simply what we have personally to make ourselves presentable in our employments or lifestyles.

Recognize too, the fact or reality that this ownership we claim may have at some time in the past been like or similar to a possession the homeless person now before us owned...and lost...and wants to recapture it and the status he/she once had...again.

Most homeless people who had a place in the community want it back.

That's been my experience over these many years of working with homeless people.

CENSUS

Let's discuss a census of a homeless population anywhere, i.e., large city, small town, medium size village and what it can do for the locale it is taken in, as well as a suggestion of how to do a census plus why it can be useful.

One of the best ways to take a census is to do it all in one day, preferably completed in daylight with volunteers and security personnel within talking distance of the volunteer census takers.

Go to the parks and similar areas at or before sunrise, then survey the streets and lastly the shelters and missed places in the city.

Security people included with census volunteers are there to quiet any disturbances and to maintain an orderly, safe census.

Usually, the homeless   cooperate

and there are very few, if any confrontations. The confrontations usually occur with the scoundrels who prey on the homeless people.

It is best to select a warm day with very little chance of rain and have enough people to complete it in twelve hours or less.

Usually, it is one volunteer to one homeless person, unless a pair of significant others won't be separated or it is a woman with children who volunteer.

A census is all about counting the homeless people plus getting answers to questions which may create other services helpful to the homeless.

Questions can highlight certain missing information about the homeless person which may influence the kinds of services needed in future projects.

Such questions may enlighten the citizens in regard to why and where the

the locality can do more humanitarian efforts to assist the homeless persons, as well as identify whether the man, woman or woman with children group may require more assistance.

This census information may help the "disconnected" to become more connected with the locale's surroundings and its people.

Certainly, a census well done can be valuable to those committees studying services for the homeless people and considering programs and projects to benefit the homeless population.

Answers to a census questionnaire may assist the City, Township, Village, urban or rural area, as well as other groups and/or agencies such as churches, organizations, government, non-profits, businesses and other entities to coordinate their efforts more effectively to the betterment of programs for the homeless population.

If the suggested census questionnaire can't be used partially or in its entirety during a census, then use it when interviewing homeless people who are applying for a homeless program or project.

Its use enhances success in program goals for the homeless populations who want to stop being homeless.

Suggested questions for the homeless person could include:

- Do you wish to remain homeless?
- Or, would you prefer to get back into the community with employment and/or education?
- Are you a permanent resident of the city turned out by relatives during the summer, fall and spring with some support during the winter months?

- Would you prefer to stay homeless, something like the old "Hobo" of a by-gone era?
- Are you a Veteran and/or a disabled Veteran of the Armed Forces of the United States?
- Are you drifting through the City and are stopping here until the next ride exiting the city?
- Are you a single man?
- Are you a single woman?
- Are you a woman with children? How many children? Their ages?
- How long have you been homeless?
- How long have you been in the City?
- How did you arrive in the City?

- Would you be willing to be reconnected with your relatives somewhere else in America in the lower connected States by achieving assistance in the future to travel by some transportation there if available, with the condition that you'll not return to this City unless you are gainfully employed?
- Have you used any of the City's agencies for help? Which ones?
- Have you used any of this State's agencies for help? Which ones?
- Have you used any of the Federal agencies for assistance? Which ones?

- What other agencies have you used or that have helped?
- Do you sleep well at night? How do you keep warm? During the day? At night?
- Do you have any way to wash your clothes? How?
- How many meals do you eat in a day? In a week?
- What do you eat for a usual meal? Where do you find meals or food?
- How often are you hungry? During a day? During a week?
- Is your food mainly a snack? Larger meals than a snack? How many meals do you eat each week?
- Do you ever eat at an organization which serves one or more meals each

week? How many meals?
- Do you ever get a chance to shower or bathe? How often? Where?
- How is your health? Are you taking a prescribed medicine? Regularly?
- Can you read?
- Do you need eye glasses to see or to read?
- Can you drive a vehicle? Car? Truck? Stick shift or automatic? Need glasses to drive?
- Do you have an ID?
- Are your feet comfortable?
- Do you need to lose weight? Gain weight?
- What is your highest grade in school?
- Did you finish eighth grade?

- Did you finish high school? Diploma? GED?
- Do you have some college? How much? Any degrees from college? In what field or discipline?
- What kind of employment or work would you like to do?
- Do you have manners?
- Do you have ethics?
- What would help you the most right now, if it were available?

The foregoing questions are offered as suggestions. Each question is designed to provide answers which may offer ideas as to the type of project to be created to assist the homeless population to a more productive life.

It may be that during a census, the organization with which the reader, you, is volunteering with or working for may use all of the suggested questions, some of them or none of them because it prefers to count only the numbers of the homeless population which exist in a particular locale on a certain day because of limited census takers.

Most cities et al will do an annual census, usually in the summer.

Townships, villages and smaller cities which haven't or don't believe they have much of a homeless population or haven't a homeless program usually will use a census to be aware of the number of homeless persons in their territorial limits, i.e., to determine since the last census if a homeless population has changed in any meaningful way.

At times the homeless census is so small that a combined effort between several towns and small communities is necessary to produce an effective program with one or more communities providing services, as well as transportation to the services offered.

Small pilot or continuing projects can often be funded by appropriate grants.

I've worked with homeless who in their past were MD's, PhD's, MS', MA'S, BS'S, BA'S, high school graduates, GED'S, those barely out of eight grade and some not past third or fourth grade.

Find the level of education a homeless person has and designing a meaningful program/project to end his/her homelessness will be more helpful and effective for that person.

PAST SIMILARITIES

A Pilot program for re-entering society/the community using education and employment results in hope and concrete action for a homeless person to act as an independent individual who is an asset to the community when homelessness ends.

This is a better result than a hopeless homeless person who recycles repeatedly in a circle of events that traps him/her to remain dependent on society and the community...forever in a despondent environment with no opportunity to end homelessness.

Regardless of whatever town, city or village exists or wherever its location, it appears there are usually homeless people who are dependent on minimal and random, yet uncoordinated help to survive as they continue their life in a hopeless environment fraught with danger.

Homeless men and women recycle daily, weekly, monthly, yearly in a life in despair, spending most of their time looking for food daily, as well as for a safe place to sleep which offers security from attack.

They continually have nothing for their hygiene, clothing replacement and other necessities plus their health is in continual disrepair as they live their life in squalor.

Have they always been this way?
NO!

Once they walked or drove to work and earned various incomes for a variety of employment, perhaps even enjoyed some educational opportunities and others may have enjoyed a family life which depended on a spouse's income.

Their life may have deteriorated over time because of financial degradation such as stock market losses or loss of physical integrity due to alcohol, excessive use of prescription drugs in the wrong way or use of illicit substances or a host of other reasons which caused them to essentially "give up" and/or get distracted from life and their welfare.

Knowing the reason for their slip may be helpful and getting that information using the previous questions suggested in the Census Chapter may be of assistance.

So, when a program/project is created to assist the homeless person to return to the community and its society with hope, employment and correction of deficiencies which hinder work, learning to have a healthy diet and exercise, along with an educational environment plus a safe place to sleep and relax, then that program/project is important.

It can be a reality created by people and communities who care.

Most homeless individuals want to change and get away from their homeless life!

Then too, some are going to have prison or jail time in their records either because of committing some felony or misdemeanor. Yet in some localities the homeless may have been arrested because a law existed to arrest them if homelessness is classified as vagrancy.

Those who have such arrest records can be more difficult to place in employment. However, it can be done with assurances which most employers will accept such as a bond to cover the employer should a loss to their business occur due to the homeless person recently hired.

There was an opportunity to acquire a $5,000 bond for such an employee to protect the employer in such a hiring situation at no cost to either the employee or the employer.

So, incarceration isn't the employment discouragement of past times.

Another service that can be provided to the homeless is one of showing up in court when clients come before a judge for parole or some infraction which might send them to jail.

It was a service I started in one community by presenting it to the respective judge and asking the judge if the man or women stayed with my program and worked with me in their homeless program, could they remain out of jail?

I suggested to the judge that in whatever time frame, i.e., one, two or three months, the client and I could return to the court to explain the progress the client had made since the last time we appeared before the judge.

Most judges told the client as long a they stayed in my program and worked with me, the client would remain under my supervision.

Each judge stipulated when each future court appearance would be and he/she expected a full report on the activities of the respective client and we both were expected to attend that hearing. Each report was to include any work the client had performed, as well as any education completed or in progress.

If the client left my program for any reason, he/she was required to report to the court the reason for leaving and the judge would decide the fate of the client.

This ancillary program was a helpful and successful opportunity for many clients. Clients were represented in court by the Public Defender's Office in that locale.

The ancillary court program proved by employment and education that both previously incarcerated individuals and those who hadn't had the experience can capture education and employment, as well as improve their life plus acquire the necessities of life.

The result was a successful return to the community and its society with respect.

During these years of working with homeless clients there were numerous "pay phones" scattered in various places in most cities, towns, and villages, whether small or large.

Every client I had in larger cities, I gave "free" two quarters which would activate a telephone so the client in difficulty could call me at home or the office anytime, day or night, to tell me of his/her problem or concern.

When I couldn't solve the difficulty

by phone, I'd ask the location of the client and go find him/her in the city, regardless of the night's hour or in the daytime or ask him/her to come to the office.

When I located the client after office hours, we usually went to a 24 hour Diner in the shabbier part of the city, ate and talked.

For some reason, I was never hurt or attacked wherever I went, even in the ghettos. And, this was the situation wherever I worked. Reader, this situation applied only to me and is not meant to apply to you automatically because you assist the homeless.

Always be aware of your surroundings!

VOLUNTEERING SUGGESTIONS

Whether you work or volunteer with an organization or you contribute your time individually before beginning, it is necessary to select the kind of homeless people you'll focus on unless the organization, such as a non-profit, has pre-selected and currently is working with only men or women or women with children.

Few entities or shelters work with all three types of homeless individuals in the same shelter area because shelters aren't constructed usually to separate men, women and women with children.

However, the discussion in the last chapter of this book could change, if adopted, that past philosophy due to the external security suggested which could keep all types separated, yet in the same residence area for the project.

Different personal needs may be

required, however the deficiencies may be similar for men, women and/or women with children.

Serving homeless persons of both genders simultaneously can occur when the service rendered is the provision of food, counseling, education and similar types of services, yet not for sheltering unless the shelter has separation and security to enforce the separation. Otherwise chaos is likely the result.

Most counselors can assist both men and women, albeit some are specific only for men or for women or women with children.

When working for an organization, whomever it has contracted to serve will be your work as a staff member. Same requirements are for the volunteer.

Whether you work in the homeless service or volunteer or act as an individual assisting homeless people on your own with whatever specialty is thought to be noble by you, be aware that there are hazards sometimes on the street.

Be aware of your surroundings whether you are in a group or by yourself.

Be alert to potential dangers when you are out there.

On the street is not a tourist walk in the park nor is it a picnic, regardless of how wonderful your intentions are.

The longer you work with homeless people in their environment, the easier it gets, yet we who are on the street are always alert to the people around us and the general surroundings.

Initially, and almost all the time you'll be in the organization's facility, so you won't be on the street often unless where you volunteer or work is in the midst of skid-row, the slums or a ghetto.

There are times when you walk to your volunteer work, you'll see a fifty or hundred dollar bill on the sidewalk. My advice is to walk on by and ignore it because often tough men and/or women are hiding out of sight nearby.

When you bend over to pick the money up, they slam you against a nearby car, strip you of your pants and shorts if you are a man or pull your skirt or dress and panties off. Then, take your purse and flee while you try to cover yourself, stagger and hurt bad!

The thieves also pick up their money on the sidewalk as they run off.

Remember, muggings, theft, beatings and other incidents can occur day and night in certain large cities, as well as in smaller towns and cities.

If you wish to help homeless people by yourself, until you are used to the street, it is better to put word out on the street that you'll see homeless men or women or women with children at an office setting.

So, use a nearby church and rent some space or get an office near where you want to work.

Should you insist to work alone in the slums, it is suggested you work with an organization first to get some experience if you've never had any working with homeless people. You'll appreciate what you learn and it will be useful in the future.

Always be aware and alert to your surroundings anywhere at any time.

Some religious seminaries give their men and women students exposure to street work helping homeless men and women and the poor. However these students are in the street in groups for protection. Street homeless people are usually interested in the groups and what services they offer.

The religious groups benefit as well because they meet the homeless and the poor in their residence or lack of it.

Also, the religious groups get experience working with people who are different than they. Those who will have churches, mosques, synagogues or other meeting places won't be as likely to panic when a disheveled, smelly person comes to worship...and the spiritual leader may have some solutions to the person's problems.

One night several years ago while working in a large city, I was making some rounds in the skid-row district. As I walked by a hotel, I noticed three prostitutes sitting on the benches in front of the hotel. It was about 7 p.m. I almost didn't make rounds that night. However for some reason, I felt I had to go. Why I felt that way that night, I have no idea.

One of the ladies asked me to stop and talk. She said they'd been waiting for me and were about to ask the hotel to call me to come by. I asked her why and what did she or the others need?

She mentioned that the lady behind her was six months pregnant and she needed to get away from her pimp and all three thought I could help. It was a Friday night.

I went into the hotel and rented a room for Friday, Saturday and Sunday night with my own money, then asked all the women if they'd eaten recently? They said "yes" that for now they were ok on that score.

The pregnant lady and I went into the hotel and we went up to her room. Further, I mentioned that food would be brought to her over the weekend and for her to stay in her room, except for washing up and going to the toilet.

The hotel clerk agreed to pass on the information to other staff to keep quiet about the pregnant lady being there.

Monday, I called a convent near another skid-row section of town and talked with the Mother Superior about the pregnant lady. She agreed to house and feed the woman until she had her baby.

Then, the woman could decide to keep the child or put it out for adoption.

I told the Mother Superior I'd keep contact with the convent periodically. When the lady wanted to work, I thought I could find work for her.

The convent kept her through the birth of her child and for six months after the birth at no cost to the woman and her child.

About three months after the birth, I found a position for her at a business office sort of as a "deliverer" of message and other odd jobs in that office.

At six months, the convent found a safe place to live close to the office she worked at plus a day care for her child.

People like those in the convent, will respond to help you in various ways and sometimes in unheard of or unadvertised ways, if you will only ask for help.

Twice the remaining prostitutes contacted me about their friend and her welfare. After that I never saw or had a contact from them.

The last discussion I had with these two who brought their friend to me for help, thanked me.

They had cared enough to seek help for their friend.

Sometimes odd situations occur and you may need to make decision of whether you'll handle it or walk away.

Whatever you decide, please stay safe.

Throughout this guide will be examples of situations which have occurred and some of these solutions may be of interest to you and perhaps of use when you seek ways to help homeless men and women and possibly the women with children.

Remember you can't do everything, yet you can do something. When you find that something to do, then do it well!

Although we've mentioned shelters a bit before and will discuss some other considerations later in this guide, let's look at some factors which will impact homeless people regarding shelters.

Suppose you are a counselor with an office and homeless folks come to you for assistance in solving their homelessness.

In this situation, usually you counsel your client, then your client fends for himself/herself of where to find shelter.

When you can make an arrangement with a shelter, such as one funded by and organization or perhaps the city's for your client to stay there for a time, you've increased the chances of your client to be successful in exiting homelessness because he/she has a dry, safe place to sleep.

Sleeping inside is important to increase the progress for your client to succeed.

If the shelter serves the evening meal, the client is blessed even more. It may be the only meal of the day, yet it is an important one.

Some services to homeless people may have a smaller budget than those serving full meals, yet they may be able to provide a healthy snack or something close to a box lunch which can be obtained in the morning. If so, it will serve as an alternate to standing in a two or more hours' lunch line.

Shelters are usually monitored at all times when men or women or women with children are in the shelter.

The monitors' word is the law enforcement of the shelter.

Disturbances such as fighting are not allowed . Often both combatants are given their possessions and quickly discharged from the shelter, regardless of the time of night or the weather outside.

Without monitors inside a shelter, people would need to sleep in groups to prevent being attacked.

Outside a shelter, some individuals try sleeping a dark doorway or under some cardboard boxes in a dump area to stay warm or maybe sneak into a hotel and sleep with a friend. Sneaking into a hotel is hard to do because entry into the room areas is usually controlled by the desk manager electronically who opens the iron gate which limits coming in or leaving.

Without a ladder, few fire escapes are close enough when depressed to grab hold of and climb.   Most fire escapes end at a hotel room window. If the room occupant won't cooperate, then the climber may need to exit by the fire escape.

Other homeless persons may sleep in trees and leave these prior to the morning patrols. If caught in the trees in a park can mean jail time in some areas resulting in a record or arrest.

Homeless people sleep little outside as a rule because roving gangs and other persons will rob, "roll", and knife them for whatever the homeless person may possess. Yet often, robbery isn't the reason for the attack. Rather it is "fun" for the attacker...evening entertainment for the attacker.

So, sleep can be poor for a homeless person. The homeless call it sleeping with "one eye" open, being alert for a threat or danger.

In one large city where I worked, there were about 8000 homeless men, women and women with children and 1400 shelter beds or about one for every six or seven homeless persons. Most were for men. About 200 were for women and another 100 or so for women with children.

Other places of rest were nestled places where police patrols usually didn't find them. These people kept track of the tides and stayed there only when the morning tides didn't inundate the sleeping areas and the outgoing tides weren't a bother.

It's been mentioned about people and their kids sleeping in park trees, however it wasn't noted that most were fairly well supplied with plastic coverings to shed the heavy dew and/or often rain.

For the most part, usually the about 2300 homeless who stayed in the park each night were away from the animal enclosures and botanical gardens and were somewhat successful in getting a decent night's sleep. During the day, they wandered the city looking for food and/or soup lines.

Some of the soup or meal lines of people for free food stretched more than two blocks for more than two hours because people kept adding to the line.

Without a safe shelter or a place to shower to stay clean plus find some consistent nourishing food, it is hard, rather almost impossible for a homeless person to concentrate on a program which will change his/her life to end homelessness. There isn't time to study or learn a type of work they can do or find employment by themselves.

Helping homeless men and women

to find work is difficult because of the foregoing obstacles and the deficiencies which may surface for a particular individual.

For many homeless, particularly men, anger management courses are a necessity.

Reader, you know as I do that people who have less than desirable or acceptable hygiene, poor nourishment, disruptive sleep, wear the same tattered unwashed clothing everyday aren't likely to be accepted in the workforce by employers.

Often, the knowledge of how to work in a particular field may be absent because from grade school to through high school, if the person went that far, they may not have learned the ethics of the workplace nor the skills for employment.

To gain the workplace requires some education, now including computer skills, to find work. Those deficiencies merged with some locales arresting homeless people for being homeless or vagrant in some places decrease work and study opportunities particularly if they have a "criminal record" due to arrests.

Consequently, the misery increases as does the hopelessness.

Many times the misery is so great around holidays, especially Christmas Eve, the homeless people will give up and commit suicide.

In fact, Christmas Eve is the day of the year on which most homeless persons will attempt or choose to end their life by suicide.

To thwart some of these suicides, every year when I had the funds, I gave a Christmas Eve or as close to Christmas Eve party with food and a gift for everyone for as many attendees as I could invite and afford.

Sometimes other persons so inclined gave some food or funds into the pot and we had fun serving the homeless men, women and women with children and sharing for a few hours.

After the party, those who could and wished to, were invited to a Christmas Eve service in a chapel or area which could be used as a chapel or where we had the party.

Often for these parties, I had help from the homeless men and women who were cooks and could help me in the kitchen, church fellowship hall in setting up tables and chairs or decorating.

Then too, sometimes non-homeless people volunteered to pitched in to help, as well.

For me, and I suspect for others, it was a joy to watch homeless and non-homeless people sharing the fun of wrapping Christmas gifts for the party.

My helpers, i.e., everyone who

helped me as staff got a present, too which only I wrapped. There was a present for homeless and non-homeless alike.

They weren't aware that they would get a Christmas present until the time the party guests were each, adults and children alike, given their presents.

Party sizes varied from year to year and depended on my budget. The smallest party was about ten and the largest was 150 guests not counting the helpers.

My helpers stayed to help me clean up the debris...and everyone who helped I invited to breakfast that either I cooked in the church kitchen or made a deal at some 24 hour diner to fix us breakfast on Christmas morning.

When all had left and I had only to lock up, there was a quiet time...and a few moments of peace. Sometimes new thoughts of how to help homeless people came to me.

As I went home, I was thankful that I wasn't homeless.

I was tired after a party, maybe almost exhausted and probably the rest of the volunteers were experiencing a similar feeling. When I lay down to sleep, it came quickly.

It may be of interest to note that the free breakfast I provided on Christmas morning was for everyone who helped, homeless and non-homeless alike...and most of them ate two to three times what I could put away for breakfast.

We'd talk during breakfast and afterwards for a while. Then, we'd part with Christmas wishes and blessings for all plus my thank you to everyone...and a personal Christmas card for each person.

One year, I worked for a non-profit as a consultant, mentor and team member for their homeless program for men.

My area assignment was primarily with the homeless men and the challenge to get the menfolk back into society with employment where possible.

This organization operated a shelter at night for men in the midst of skid row.

In the days leading up to Christmas, I was placed in charge of getting people to ring bells for hanging "red pots" for donations from the general public and whoever wished to put money in the pot outside of stores and other businesses.

The city was a west coastal city and with its wind and humidity during December, thin clothing made working outside even more of a challenge.

The Director of the non-profit I worked for wasn't too keen on my choice of people to ring bells for Christmas donations by hiring only homeless men and women.   After considerable discussion, some of it rather terse, he said that hiring these homeless people would be ok, however the responsibility was mine and mine alone for the donation outcome.

I said, "Fine...let's get at it"!

As I hired my donation staff, I managed to obtain heavy winter coats and other clothing plus some gloves for some that wanted such.

After getting permission from the store or business for the bell ringing during store hours plus permission for them to use the staff bathroom, I placed every man or woman strategically throughout the city.

I gave each bell ringer a sack lunch, if they wanted one for the first week shift which began when the store or business opened until the store closed or I picked them up and collected their pots.

Then, I took the workers to wherever in the city they wished to be let off for the evening plus a box lunch if they wished one for a couple of days.   .

However, most walked out of the non-profit door and disappeared, then all returned for work early the next morning on time.

Fortunately, I found a small short order restaurant to make the lunches and snacks for me for pickup prior to meeting with the crew.

I paid for the lunches and snacks for the crew and didn't mention that fact to my employer. The non-profit never had furnished food to any of the workers in the past.   And, I assumed it wasn't about to change its policy.

In my pot crew was a retired homeless Army Sergeant. The way he helped me handle the crew and his mannerisms prompted me to think he was a former Master Sergeant. It was obvious he had combat experience. He was wonderful help to me because throughout the day he walked or bussed to every bell ringer at least once daily to check and learn if everything was ok. When he saw me at the office or on the street, he gave me information as to how each bell ringer was doing and if they needed anything.

Bell ringers were working from the Friday after Thanksgiving to Christmas Eve. There were several bell ringers during that time that required an empty pot supplied to them because their pot was full before their shift was over.

When I had to pick up a full pot and replace it with an empty one, Sarge stayed with the bell ringer until I could get there. Often, he exchanged the pots with me, so I didn't need to get out of my car. After we'd take the filled pot to the office and lock it up, I'd drop him at whatever bell ringer was next in line.

The bell ringers worked seven days weekly.

Every Friday after their shift was over, they were paid by check or in cash by the non-profit according to the number of hours worked from the previous Friday through the payroll week of Thursday. Overtime was frown on, yet it was paid.

With Sarge's help, I kept in touch with every bell ringer, so that when their area slowed or stopped in donations, they were moved to more crowded areas to better the donations.

Every day between the two of us, we kept in communications with every bell ringer at least twice a day and more often than that most of the time.

I met a fellow at the non-profit one day who manufactured what he called "Promise Cards" which he made as either a religious card or a business card with easy to understand wise thoughts printed inside on each card with a beautiful scene on the back of the card.

To read the thought, the card needed to be opened.

This guy had worked on making the cards and marketing them for over two years to churches and businesses.

It was such a new idea that businesses and churches were slow to learn the value of the cards, as well as to figure out how to use the card for a benefit...it probably was about a decade ahead of its time.

I thought it a marvelous idea, so I suggested a marketing idea using the homeless bell ringers to distribute the card to each individual who donated to the red pots.

He'd never heard of hiring homeless people to be bell ringers, yet he thought it was an exciting idea and something quite different!

The manufacturer liked the idea and gave me several thousand cards free for the homeless bell ringers to give out to the people donating to the pots.

Sarge and I left a thousand cards with each bell ringer with the reminder we could get more when they ran out. Most of the bell ringers said that when they gave out the card and the folks read them, some came back to give another donation, so they could get another card.

As I recall, we gave out over 20,000 cards and the bell ringers mentioned that folks donating really liked the cards and years later I remember eating at a restaurant and buying something at a pharmacy...and what was taped to the cashier counter in both places...it was one of the cards given out by the bell ringers that Christmas.

Seeing both cards sorta gave my heart's strings...a tug!

Close to Christmas Sarge and I stopped at the public ice skating rink in center city. We set up two tripods with a red pot on each, one for each of us and started ringing bells to draw a donation crowd.

In about two or so hours, we gave out over 3000 cards. The crowd grew to more than a two block line for both of our lines.

Several police showed up to learn if there was a problem or demonstration because there were so many people in one place next to the skating rink on its square.

When the police decided there wasn't a riot, most of them left. However, a couple of officers stayed until we were through. We gave the police officers some cards too plus some for the fellows at the station.

Word apparently got around the city that certain bell ringers had something new and free for a donation and the donations climbed.

Then, the last bell ringing day came.

It was Christmas Eve. We quit about 5:30 p.m. and in two loads, I took everyone back to my office and we locked up the red pots and bells.

Albeit, every day I turned in the money collected, yet this day when I turned the final amount of money I had a hunch we'd done very well!

I asked all the bell ringers to follow me to a room I'd reserved and as they entered there was surprise on their faces.

"Come and sit and share a Christmas Eve dinner together before you go.", I suggested.

We all sat on the hardwood floor and took off our warm jackets. They all looked around the room at the buckets of food, beverages and deserts.

There was a Christmas tree of lights

and ornaments with presents all around the base of the tree.

Tears of joy streaked many faces.

During dinner small talk abounded and included their experiences of bell ringing.

Some asked if the jackets I'd gotten them to work in had to be returned...and I told the to keep the jackets, thermal underwear and gloves.

When dinner was over, each bell ringer was given a gift wrapped in a different colored wrapping and tied with ribbons. The men were excellent rippers. Ladies were gentler and apparently planned to save the wrapping paper and ribbon, so they were slower finding what their gift was.

Eventually, all talking stopped. Silence drifted in.

Over the years, I learned that during these silence times it is best to wait because something unusual is likely to come.

It did.

One of the ladies looked at everyone and at me...waited...then said, "Herb, I might as well start this off. This is the first Christmas Eve in thirty years that I haven't by this time of day been thoroughly...drunk...completely polluted ...and I'm only 42."

The rest unloaded their life hesitantly, yet all were pretty much drunk on Christmas Eve for lesser years plus they were despondent.

A couple of the crew, a man and a woman had contemplated suicide this Christmas Eve.

Several said they were pleasantly shocked this Christmas Eve because leading up to it, they had and been paid weekly for their services, been trusted with some pretty fair amounts of money without close supervision, were tired yet happy, been wonderfully and unexpectedly fed and surprised with a gift for Christmas.

We cleaned up the ripped paper and supper leavings. Then, I gave them their last payment for the current and last week of their employment plus a Christmas card to each of them from me.

Each said goodnight, the door closed and they left, leaving me alone with my thoughts.

A few minutes later, there was an unexpected knock on the door. I opened it...and there stood the whole group.

"Is there something you wanted?" I asked.

The lady who started the discussion said, "Herb, we decided to give you a special present on this Christmas Eve...something you probably haven't had before."

A few minutes ago, we agreed to "buddy" with each other and keep our buddy and ourselves from doing something foolish like drinking, becoming despondent and hopeless or committing suicide this Christmas Eve and throughout the holidays and into the New Year. That is your Christmas present from us."

I hugged and thanked each one of them...and they left. They left me with another Christmas present which they didn't know about...and that was several tears of joy!

Some I never saw again, although I heard most of them made good on their getting back into the community and its society. A few of them did eventually come to me and apply to be in the homeless men's program I was counseling.

Occasionally, my memories surface

and I remember that Christmas Eve and many others...fondly!

Anyone reading this Practical Guide can do the same as I did...and probably even better!

Regarding the bell ringers donation collections, about a week later I learned that our homeless team had placed this non-profit in first place in its division with its family of non-profits scattered throughout the city. Our non-profit was in dingy skid-row in the city and it had never placed that high in the history of the red donation pots in the city.

In fact, our non-profit in all of its history had always placed last in money collected.

The Director of our non-profit was more than surprised...he was flabbergasted...and complemented highly at his organizational Directors' meeting after Christmas by the President of the non-profit organization.

Our Director was stunned and as happy as I'd ever seen him.

Secretly, I was pleased with how well the homeless bell ringers had performed...to be honest, I was overjoyed!

Working with homeless people isn't easy most of the time. Yet, the experiences you collect will give you a great heap of "warm fuzzys" or good feelings that you'll have forever. Plus, when you help a homeless person regain a worthy place in society which is safe and has hope, albeit you may never meet that individual again, you'll always remember. Those thoughts will give you inner warmth wherever you go.

For the homeless, you are and will be their "Good Samaritan" who didn't pass by, rather tarried to help.

Regardless of how much effort we input to our homeless programs or projects, we lose some. I've lost some, yet fortunately they were very few.

When you wonder what the homeless men and women are like, remember most of them were like you are now.

They had homes as you have, yet for some reason, often financial they lost all they had including their family or wife or husband and ended up on the street of despair with little or no hope or knowledge of regaining a respected place in the community.

Some are going to be veterans. Others will be like your neighbors next door and some you'll meet you've never met.

Currently most homeless people, unless they are in a program with mostly complete services, tend to recycle daily with hopelessness even with the provided food lines, a shelter for maybe a night or two, yet they constantly look all day for their needs of the day with no end in sight.

Until this practical guide you're reading, there apparently hasn't been a guide with suggestions to show cities, governments and other organizations a way to give the homeless a pathway to stop being homeless and find a way back into the community and its society as an independent, self-supporting individual.

IDEAS TO HELP
HOMELESS PEOPLE
WIN

Granted the charity programs help a person for a moment in time, yet that isn't enough.

Yes, we need to keep those programs because they do some good. Still what is needed is to create projects which give hope and inspiration to those homeless men, women and women with children who wish to return to the community and society.

This idea will be discussed in depth later in this guide.

So, if you want to try to learn or experience what it is like to be homeless, try giving up everything you see or have for eight hours or perhaps 16 hours or maybe a full 24 hours.

By each or any of these time

periods, you'll have a good idea of what a homeless person needs in that time frame...they need everything!

As a suggestion, when formerly homeless people left my programs for work and/or education, they often asked that when they got to making money could they make a donation or pay me for the help they received?

I asked each person who offered to pay me for my services, as well as everyone who successfully left my program to, when they were financially stable and their mind set was also well established, to go out and do something for a homeless man or woman.

An example might be buying the person a dinner or giving them some food or a bus pass or a warm bedroll or something they thought would help the homeless person.

My philosophy was that when they helped a person this way, then they could consider me well paid for my help and services to them when they were homeless.

Later in this guide, you'll learn what some did and when they found me again what happened. These successful, formerly homeless men and women told me their story, either in person or by phone what they had done for a homeless man or woman.

In addition to the good feeling, they captured something else unexpected which many homeless will disclaim they have and that is compassion!

When a homeless person was accepted as my client, I gave each client two quarters of my own money plus my office and my home phone with the suggestion that they could call any time during the day or night from any pay phone scattered throughout the city when things weren't going well and they felt they were in trouble.

Whenever a homeless person called and we couldn't solve their predicament over the phone, I asked them where they were and went to their location, often driving back into the city in the middle of the night at 2 or 3 a.m. to find the person and pick him/her up.

Usually, at that time I took them to an all-night diner to eat or get a cup of coffee and talk. After we talked and the homeless person was in better spirits, I asked them, if it was a weekday, to come to my office in the afternoon.

When we finished talking, if there was time, I went home to bed.

In one large city of about 800,000 people, I could go anywhere in the city, including the ghettos and skid-row, unarmed without being stopped or harmed at any time of day or night.

That fact was a blessing and useful in extracting homeless clients who called.

However reader, it is suggested that you don't go into difficult areas of the city or elsewhere until you are comfortable in the area and surroundings you plan to work and have some experience in such areas.

Wherever you are, please be aware of the surroundings and people around you at all times.

When I first arrived in that city of 800,000, a friend of mine whom I'd known for more than twenty years lived in a nearby suburb. Neither of us had a job.

Yet, we both had some savings and we were interested in experimenting with and trying our theories of how to help homeless men and women we encountered to stop being homeless and go back into the community employed or doing something else constructive.

We talked with an owner of a hotel in the skid-row district of the Mission district. His hotel had several floors and no elevator. Entrance to the hotel upper rooms required passage through a steel gate electronically controlled by the shift night and day managers. It was the only access to the hotel upper room floors.

Rooms could be rented by the night, week or month and were paid in advance. All rooms had a dead-bolt lock with one key to each room. If two people shared a room, a second key could be rented for a dollar for the time of the stay.

Men and women were housed on each floor with no separation of genders. Bathrooms were labeled for men and women, as were the showers.

Room rent was fairly low.

Each floor had a monitor. When a commotion couldn't be quelled by the floor monitor or several monitors working together, police responded quickly and violators usually spent one or more nights in jail plus were suspended from the hotel and only allowed back at the owner's discretion.

My partner and I made a deal with the owner to rent the entire second floor for a month at a time to start our own homeless project of returning men and women to the community and its society.

Except for one or two persons who were given the opportunity to move or be included in our project, the second floor was unrented. The fellows became part of our project and stayed in their current rooms.

The first month we filled about half of the rooms, yet paid for all the rooms empty or filled.

Our homeless clients placed in the rooms did not pay for the room they occupied.

Beginning the second month, we had a visitor who was a member of the board of directors of one of the local non-profits which serviced homeless people in one of their job finding programs.

He wanted to contract with us for some rooms for those homeless in the non-profit's programs to serve as a consistent shelter, subject to our rules. The non-profit would pay us for the rooms used.

We agreed.

Also, we helped a couple of other non-profits the same way for a short time.

The first non-profit that contracted for rooms sent us four guys and a couple of ladies that their counselor had difficulty with and we were able to provide both a room, as well as get the homeless clients on tract with their non-profit's program.

We managed to settle the men and women down so they would embrace their non-profit's program and work with it.

After a year, when we'd finished our research and closed our program in the hotel, the same board of director's member from the first non-profit asked me if I'd like to work with the non-profit helping homeless people succeed?

He also mentioned the non-profit wasn't doing well with the homeless portion of their program and they needed help. I accepted and retired after ten years of successful work with that non-profit.

Still the only person in the Homeless Service Department, on my retirement, the non-profit I worked for was fulfilling

151% of its contracts for getting homeless people employment and education for their clients.

My partner in our research found an excellent position in another field closer to his suburban home shortly before the close of our research experiment.

Our experimentation was very successful for helping homeless men and women find their way back into the community and society plus most of them agreed to help a homeless person once their financial stability and mindset about their respective lives were secure.

Albeit our methods for helping homeless people to quit being homeless were different than that used then in the city, they worked well.

For our own clients, we corrected their deficiencies that would prohibit our clients from working. Those who didn't have a high school diploma, we made a deal with the local collage to have some of the homeless attend college to get their high school equivalent degree: the GED.

When the Dean of the college learned what we were doing with the homeless in our experiment, she allowed our clients to attend high school subjects' classes without charge. She charged it off as an experiment and we gave her some data on those homeless in regards to their respective successes or failures.

During our second floor hotel experiment, my friend and I walked around the perimeter of the second floor at random hours during the day and night plus sometimes early in in the morning.

We reserved one rented room for our office and when necessary, at times either of us slept there plus we used it to individually talk with our clients.

Our successes soon spread through the homeless population and within about six weeks we had more applicants than we had rooms for, so we had a waiting list.

When starting a program for each client, we explained that we would have rules they'd need to follow, however we would be fair, yet strict. It was explained that this was a test procedure to learn if this approach to helping homeless people could be successful. As it turned out, it was very successful.

Some of our rules included that if we found a person drunk or on drugs, we'd put them back on the street, clean up their room and give someone else an opportunity.

Also, noise beyond their door or walls would result in a warning. If it occurred again in the same day or week, we'd discharge the person from the project.

Some of the fellows we took in outweighed my partner and me perhaps by a hundred pounds. Their hundred or so extra pounds wasn't fat...it was muscle. Most knew how to use a knife or some martial art or something else to protect themselves or cause harm to someone who was trying to hurt them.

For all the homeless clients we had in those hotel rooms, neither my partner nor I were ever bothered or threatened by our clients.

STIMULATING COMPASSION

One day, I was at the college and one of my women clients was moving from class to class rather quickly.

She ran down the concrete stairs, missed a step and fell, breaking her arm above the elbow. Then, ran screaming in panic for the front door I was later told.

Several of us heard her screaming.

A couple of guys, also my clients, took off after her. One went one way and the other moved quickly in a different direction.

We all arrived at the front door about the same time, only to see her getting into a taxi and being whisked away.

I alerted the police, however I had no idea where she'd gone. I think all of us hoped she'd traveled to an emergency room.

The two guys jumped in my car and I drove to the hotel and waited. Once there, they went on about their business.

About three or four hours later, I heard a bus stop outside and looked out. She was getting out of the bus with a cast from her shoulder to her hand with a support attached.

I went downstairs and helped her upstairs to her room and into bed, covering her with blankets. She was tired. However, before she went to sleep, I asked her for the room door key.

She'd lost the key.

The day shift manager refused to call a locksmith and refused to allow me to get a locksmith until the hotel owner could be reached. The owner was out of town for a couple of days.

What to do?

I knew I couldn't stay 24 hours a day to feed her and protect her plus she needed a bland diet with lots of fluid in small amounts, like a broth for a few days.

If she was left alone, she could be raped, injured or possibly killed if somebody from the street paid some money to whomever the night manager was and came through the electronic gate or it could be someone going to or coming from the upper hotel floors stopping in for the same purposes.

She, in her present state, was defenseless.

So, I walked down the hall and knocked on two doors. Fortunately both men clients, the same two who came with me from the college, were in their rooms.

They each weighed about 315 to 325 pounds...all muscle...no fat...big bruisers. One we'd just gotten off alcohol and the other off cocaine.

I asked them, if I furnished the groceries, hot plate and refrigerator, would they each take a twelve hour shift to protect her with the broken arm, feed her, give her a sponge bath to take her temperature down, and make sure she took her medicine?

Each one looked at me and basically said the same thing: "NO!" "I'm not a nursemaid. And, I'm not compassionate. I look out for number one, I'm not like you," said both Pete and Jim (not their real names).

"Tough!" said I.

"I can't do this 24 hours a day and keep the project going. I'll toss in groceries for you, so you can cook her meals and get some food and steaks for you guys. Both of you can cook because you've done some short order cook work, so now's the time to get some practice.

"And, when was the last time either of you had steaks or prime rib or...?

"You know as well as I, once her condition gets mouthed all over the street, she probably will get raped, beaten and maybe killed...and she's part of this group you're in...so, earn your keep!

"How about trying it for a week, then we'll see what can be done. You know since she's been discharged, she can't go back to the hospital and she doesn't have any protection, except for both of you...and I don't think anybody's going to mess with either of you...not very long anyway.

"You tell me what groceries you want and I'll furnish them, starting right now!

"Which of you wants the day shift and who wants the night shift?"

"All right Herb, I'll take the night shift," volunteered Jim. Pete can, if it's ok with him, take the day shift. Here's my grocery list, got yours Pete?"

"Yeah, we'll try it. Any visitors, except you or your partner, Herb, we'll discourage 'em!"

"OK, I'll be back in a little over two hours with the groceries for both of you plus her. The refrigerator and hot plate should be delivered to the hotel in about an hour. The day manager said he'd let you know when either arrives. They may both come in the same pickup. Bring them upstairs to the room when they come, will you?

"I really appreciate your help. I'll take both of you, and your dates if you have them, out to dinner when this is through!"

Long about 8 a.m. the next day I came to the hotel and knocked on the lady's door. Jim opened the door and mentioned that Pete would take over about 9 a.m. and Jim would start his evening shift again at 9 p.m.

I asked Jim if he had any visitors last night and he said there was a guy who opened the door without knocking and walked in about two steps before he met Jim.

"Did the guy leave peacefully?", I asked.

Jim said, "Well sort of. I picked the fellow up by the back of his jacket and carried him to the stairs without the guy's feet touching the floor.

"He asked to be put down which I did at the top of the stairs. Apparently, he missed the first three steps, however he seemed to recover on the fourth step toward the gate.

"He ran down the rest of the stairs toward the iron gate yelling to the manager to let him out. The night manager let the guy out through the gate and the last I saw of him was to watch him scurrying down the street.

"I don't think he'll be back."

Continuing, Jim said he didn't think anyone else would be bothering her.

To make sure, Jim went down stairs to have a talk with the night hotel manager who told him the incident wouldn't happen again on his shift and he'd pass the message on to the oncoming shift managers.

Jim was right throughout the whole period of several weeks in that he and Pete didn't have any more unwanted visitors.

As the lady healed, got her strength back, could walk around, she was ready for a shower and then to see the doctor.

Jim's and Pete's girlfriends took the lady into the hotel shower in the morning and stayed in the shower with her so she could shower safely, dried her, then dressed her and brought the lady to her room.

Pete and Jim fixed lunch for us.

Afterwards, Pete and his girlfriend left, leaving Jim and his girlfriend to go with me and the lady to see her physician.

The doctor decided to have the lady return next week to have her cast removed.

So, the next week while Pete and I took her to the hospital, Jim and his girlfriend plus Pete's girlfriend got reservations for a "cast coming off" party for the six of us at a nearby restaurant complete with a "reverent" ceremony for presenting the lady with her room key.

We all took her to her room.

She thanked us all and as we left, we heard the inside door bolt turn in its place locking the door of the lady's room.

That was a pleasant sound we had all waited for...and we sighed in unison in relief that she now was well and in charge of her life again.

It was a job well done...for two fellows who protested that they didn't have an ounce of compassion.

A couple of weeks later I found a job for Jim and after his first paycheck, he left the project.

The lady finished her time with the project and went to work in the business office of a local hotel outside the skid-row area. She moved out of the project hotel and the program after her second paycheck.

A few years later, I was standing downtown on the street corner waiting for a stoplight to change so I could walk across a street, when someone tapped me on the shoulder. I turned around and here was this lady who broke her arm. She was very stylishly dressed.

She said to me, "Herb, I know you forget our names deliberately when we leave the project so you won't greet us, unless we first greet you because some of us may have important jobs where having been homeless might not be helpful on our resume'.

"It's been a few years since I've seen you, however I just wanted to thank you again for all your help. I see Jim once in a while and he's doing real well. And, that was something you did for Pete at the church before he went to his cooking job after Thanksgiving a few years ago.

"I'm now the Manager of a major hotel in the city and I enjoy my work. My husband was the boyfriend you helped when he came home from prison. He's now an Assistant Manager of a different hotel in the city and he likes his work. He even had a recent promotion.

"Last year we got to a point where we thought ourselves to be stable in our heads and in money, so we helped a homeless man working with a project to complete it and find work.

"And, you know something, you told us we'd get lots of 'warm fuzzys' or good feelings in doing so...and we did!

"We had so much fun that we thought we'd try helping a lady this year and maybe a woman with children the following year.

"My husband and I can't thank you enough. Blessings to you always! And, thank you for helping us to succeed! Oh, by the way, we asked the fellow we helped to help some homeless person in some way like you asked us to do.

" Some others you helped are doing the same as you asked us to do with the homeless, so when enough of us do this maybe the homeless numbers will decrease drastically! Oh, Oh, Gotta run!"

I watched her disappear in the crowd and I never saw her again, yet I think of her and her husband at times, along with Jim and Pete and their women friends. Those warm fuzzys will be with me always.

Returning to the time shortly before I closed the project, Pete did some more surprising things with me before he left and one of them startled me in a good way.

We closed the project a week after Thanksgiving. Pete was the last to leave the project. He helped me clean the rooms before I returned the keys to the management.

Pete went to his new cooking job during that week after Thanksgiving and was staying in a modest apartment.

The weekend before Thanksgiving, I had promised the church pastor to prepare a Thanksgiving dinner for seniors in the church, as well as the Pastor and his family. I figured it would take three turkeys to feed everyone plus serve it with all the trimmings.

So, I asked Pete if he could help me set up the tables and decorate them plus help in the kitchen doing some cooking.

A lady from the church had just returned from some cooking school learning how to prepare dinners for the congregation and other crowds, so she said she'd help us prepare the meal.

I'd cooked many dinners on their old large gas stove and used its oven a good deal, so I knew I could cook everything needed for the dinner. Usually my turkey was tender...so tender that the meat fell off the bones.

So, Pete and I showed up several hours ahead of the dinner and met the lady and asked her about her schooling as we walked to the kitchen.

When I walked through the doors to the kitchen, I was shocked because the old gas stove I cooked many meals on over the years and the antiquated appliances I'd learn to use were all gone.

In its place was a brand new convection kitchen with the latest appliances, all of which I didn't know how to use...not any of it! The stainless steel seemed to smile at me...and I started to sweat.

Now readers, you need to remember that ladies perspire...and only horses and men...sweat!

The church had installed a brand new $50,000 convection oven state of the art kitchen.

I must have looked very nervous...and to be honest very shocked because time was dwindling away and in a few hours people were going to be disappointed if dinner wasn't ready.

The lady laughed and said, "Herb, the church sent me to school to learn how to use this kitchen, so don't worry, dinner will be on time. There are a few things I'll need to experiment with, yet I think everything will work out."

I looked at Pete and started to ask him to help me with some other volunteers to set up the tables and decorations, when I saw a twinkle in Pete's eye and a smile on his face.

Pete looked at me and the lady and said, "Just as the lady says, it'll all work out because she and I'll have everything ready."

He lost me there, so I asked him what he meant?

I had a hunch I was about to learn something I didn't know about Pete and it probably wouldn't have surfaced if he wasn't helping me for the many expected people coming to celebrate Thanksgiving.

Looking at the lady, he said, "Miss, I am a Master Chef trained in the use of convection ovens and kitchens. Every appliance, oven and counter in this kitchen, I know how to use to cook the turkeys, bake the pies, prepare the salads, decorate pies, slice the turkey and anything else on the menu plus I'll teach you 'easy to use ways' of working with the kitchen they didn't teach you at school.

"If you'll let me, I'll show you how to make your first meal in this kitchen with ease and it will be superb! Herb and his helpers can decorate and set the tables while you and I enjoy your kitchen plus you'll learn some ideas you can use for your pies and pastry. Deal?"

"Deal!"

"Pete, you just took away my being nervous for this first cooking. Thank you! Where do we start?" said the lady?

"Herb, if you have any questions, just come into the kitchen and ask. Is this ok with you?" queried Pete.

"Sure. This the second time you've pulled my fat out of the fire. Thank you!"

"Yeah, well you taught me something very valuable. And, until I met you…I didn't have it!"

"What was that, Pete?" asked Herb.

"Compassion! When Jim and I took care of that injured lady 'till she healed, was that the first time I pulled your fat out of the fire?"

"Yep! OK, you two get busy cooking and we'll get the out front serving areas set up plus put out the plates, dinner-dinnerware and decorations. If you need anything, let me know."

Dinner was one of the best I've ever eaten. Sure, I can usually cook turkey tender, yet it falls off the bones. Pete's and the lady's turkey meat stayed mostly on the bones and it seemed more tender than what I could cook.

Each turkey was professionally sliced. Every pie was delicious, as were the salads and other decorated pastry. All of the meal was scrumptious!

The seniors and other people who enjoyed the dinner said it was like home cooking. Some said it tasted like their Mother cooked in the pioneer days. The Pastor and his wife really complemented Pete and the church lady who cooked with Pete for the excellent dinner and my team for the table preparedness and decorations.

Everyone appeared to enjoy dinner.

The stories you've read thus far are true, however the names are fictitious and the locations of where these events happened are not revealed.

People of various backgrounds,

education, races and cultures have many different kinds of problems which when not solved will cause homelessness in our country. And, it is time to start doing something to cure this blight.

As a volunteer or staff member, you have the opportunity to offer some of your time and energy to help these homeless people regain a respected place in the community.

Reader, I hope you will challenge homelessness wherever you find it in your community.

The next Chapter provides suggestions you may wish to use when you decide to assist the homeless persons you'll meet as you continue your search to be more effective in helping those who need your help.

SUGGESTIONS

- To learn about the services currently provided to homeless men, women, and/or women with children where you live or work, ask your friends, scout the urban and/or rural county and Federal offices plus organizations, churches and any other entity serving the homeless people. This information is useful whether you are going to volunteer or thinking of applying for employment to help homeless persons.
- A good inventory of services currently available to help the homeless eases the selection and/or development of necessary services

- Do your volunteering or employment with a clinical attitude. This means to have empathy for the homeless individual and not sympathy. The essence of it is to not get emotionally involved with the homeless client because in any profession, including medical or ancillary professions or other professions serving the public, clear thinking of how to help a person homeless or otherwise, is important and clouded or absent when one is emotionally involved with the client. More good in helping that person succeed is present when the counselor or other position assisting isn't emotionally associated with the client. Clear thinking produces better ways to end homelessness.
- Be a good listener to find out more about the homeless person and

where they wish to go or what they wish to be.

- Be friendly.
- Modification of services provided in larger populated areas may be required to give similar assistance to homeless people in lesser populated areas.
- Often, when people think of helping the homeless individually, they want to rush to the street and get started...**DON'T!** Plan what you expect to do and put in place safeguards.
- When feasible, volunteer and learn to talk with and serve homeless people before you decide to be employed to work with them.
- If you've taken a job with an organization who serves homeless and your experience of the street is limited, ask your supervisor or new

colleagues about any tips they suggest and what the usual street activity around the office is.

- Before applying for a job to work with homeless people, remember many offices are on the edge of skid-row or in the middle of it. It these locations are uncomfortable, don't apply.
- Wherever you volunteer or work, i.e., skid-row, the ghettos or the fringe of these, always be aware of your surroundings and be alert...it is a safety factor. It is a trait most people have in larger populated areas. In today's time, it appears that all of us whether our area for home or work is urban or rural have varying degrees of alertness wherever we are. If you do, it may save you some grief. If you haven't developed the trait to be always alert to your surroundings, it is

suggested you develop that awareness soon.

- You can enjoy helping homeless people make their life better plus you'll have your share of warm fuzzys or good memories which will give lasting remembrances...always...and you'll do these services most likely better than I or anyone else has previously accomplished.
- Please go help the homeless men, women and/or women with children as a volunteer or an employee or any way you can...your help is needed and appreciated!

MOST OF OUR IDEAS
TO HELP
HOMELESS PEOPLE
NEED CHANGING!

Granted, most of the "free" to the homeless services help each person a little bit yet won't end homelessness since there isn't any guidance for anyone to use as how to get back into the community and its society by stop being homeless.

The homeless folks appreciate:

- eating meals one to three times weekly,
- getting their laundry done,
- relaxing for an hour or two inside to get in out of the weather, and
- maybe getting some used clothing.

Then, they leave the facility and return to scrounging for food and shelter the rest of the day and the rest of the week. The next day is the same routine, unless another facility is available and open for a few hours.

Keep these services available for now for a moment in time because there is some relief for the homeless person...and they are grateful for it...since it is something to look forward to even though it simply recycles the homeless individual and continues to do so.

Yet, as good or helpful these organizations are, still the homeless person has little to look forward to except staying homeless.

The services these facilities provide may be all they can do because that's all the funding they have.

The communities which have these services should be encouraged to continue them, even when more thorough services which do end homelessness become available. This is because while ending homelessness for a certain number of people may occur, there still will very likely be other homeless people waiting to enter the project when there is room for them.

In essence, the usual current system of helping homeless men, women and/or women with children throughout most of the country needs coordination and cooperation of services to reduce the duplication of services which may occur at the same hour like two or more organizations serving meals at the same hour.

Stagger the hours and more people may be fed or perhaps a person can get one or two meals that day or perhaps the scheduling would permit one meal a day five or six or seven days.

One city I knew of in the United States put some methods in practice to try to help the homeless person obtain tools to gain jobs in that community and take advantage of the opportunity to be self-sufficient.

These are ideas and ways to end homelessness. I worked in one of the cities which had this concept...and it worked, albeit it was sometimes difficult because of the limited time allowed in a shelter.

The next chapter, How to End Homelessness, has a simpler more effective solution and this will be discussed in-depth.

Using that solution can end the misery of being homeless using guidance and giving inspiration to the applicant.

It isn't easy to work with homeless people, yet it is worthwhile and something we need to do.

Watching homeless people you've helped to stop being homeless, take hold of their life again and reentering the community and its society as a self-supporting person will give you a self-satisfaction you'll remember.

In the next chapter, methods for helping homeless men, women and/or women with children either as a gender specific program or a mixed genders project will be shown, illustrated and detailed in procedure and concept for you to consider in your locale.

Modify these suggested methods to your area to produce something appropriate to the homeless population you wish to assist.

Remember, homeless people are homeless for a variety of reasons and causes. They are stuck in time, plodding endlessly and being recycled daily to do the same thing continually.

They do not have the resources to get out of the homeless rut...yet you and I do know how to do this...and it may take us years to change the insufficient help given which recycles people endlessly to staying homeless.

Or it may, with adequate funding

and people like you who care, perhaps we can change nationally our methods currently in use to something practical which **stops homelessness...forever!**

Are you game?

HOW TO END HOMELESSNESS

How you can end homelessness where you are!

This discussion will illustrate an in-depth method with suggestions as a guide to end homelessness for those homeless persons who desire to do so.

It is also a guide for the reader, as an individual, or organization or government or church or non-profit who/which can use it to make appropriate modifications to address the homeless needs of a respective locale.

These suggestions can be accomplished by staff and volunteers of average to more educated backgrounds who care about guiding men or women or women with children to end the misery of homelessness.

It takes a well-designed program using common sense, compassion, patience and coordination of services.

Also is needed an understanding of the difficulties homeless people experience in order assist the homeless person to change to being self-sufficient, such as employed, return to the community and its society.

The use of certain tools (services, types of employment, education and so forth) may require being available prior to the beginning the project while other tools may be developed as the need arises.

One first concern is to know what is the problem, i.e., how many people are homeless? Are they only men or women or women with children or a combination of all three?

Before any project is designed, learn what the homeless population is, i.e., take a Census. Do it preferably in one day in daylight...and if necessary a few hours during the dark hours.

Study the previous Census chapter

for ideas and questions to ask if feasible. Numbers of homeless people are most important, yet some questions answered may assist in project design.

Take the Census with volunteers or staff or both plus security personnel such as Police Officers or Security Guards being with or nearby the Census takers.

Analyses of the data will help determine the design of the project to end homelessness in your locale.

As a suggestion, a Census should be taken at least once a year.

Develop a simple application for the homeless to apply to the ending homelessness project. Have each applicant sign the document because the acceptance into your project will be of interest and importance for each person being considered to be in the program.

Again, review the Census Chapter for ideas of questions which may be desired to use in the application.

Applicant populations may vary in size. Consequently, decide whether homeless people will be accepted as they apply and continue until the project is full or with an excess number of applicants there will be a sorting out of who will be accepted and fill the program.

Certain enrollees will progress and leave the project sooner than others, so those on a waiting list may continually be accepted when openings occur.

After selection of candidates for the program, discuss in a general assembly the rules of the program, what is allowed and what is not. Answer the questions which the applicants may ask and assure them that further questions may be answered by their counselor.

Make sure the homeless applicants understand that this is a privilege type of project funded by people and other sources who believe each homeless person should have one more chance to stop being homeless and the homeless enrollee is expected to do his/her part.

This program being offered as a privilege to help a homeless person return to the community and its society, where possible, however the program is not a right. So, when certain rules are not followed, discharge from the project may be the result.

Applicants may, at any time, notify their counselor that they wish to leave the project and they will be allowed to do so.

For a shelter, find a motel or a floor in a hotel or something equivalent to use. Should facilities which can be used as a shelter currently, use it.

Whatever is used as a shelter, such as a motel, find a manager or owner who will cooperate with the project by renting rooms on a weekly, monthly and/or annual basis plus will provide invoices for the time periods of use agreed on.

Invoices for rent periods are useful for tracking expenses for grants and other monetary reasons.

Arrange a bond to protect the project and to repair any damage to a room caused by any person connected to the program. Any client causing damage to a room or to the motel should be discharged from the project immediately. Further action is at the program's discretion.

Using a motel (or its equivalent) allows the project to have men, women and women with children in a project all at once in separate rooms, should the project be so designed with counselors and security to handle this mixed population.

Have security guards protect the project from outside intrusions, as well as preventing the men and women from sleeping together while in the project. What is decided about married couples in a project is the discretion of the program.

Remember men, women and women with children will, on occasion require different personal supplies along with certain services.

Since project enrollees have an address and can receive mail, each person can get an ID (state identification card) or a driver's license if qualified plus they can be someone who can open a savings or checking account in a bank or credit union and use it for perhaps savings.

Rooms should be cleaned by motel staff at least twice weekly or more depending on the Project Director's directive. Change of towels and bed sheets should also be considered in the clean-up times. As a suggestion, omit amenities in the room.

Room clean-up knowledge is important for the project enrollees for when they have their own place, so the Project Director may consider shifting this to the enrollee for a time as a learning experience.

As a suggestion, rent sufficient rooms for the project homeless population plus enough rooms for each project counselor to use as an office and perhaps stay overnight occasionally, as well as one or more rooms for the security guard(s) to keep warm or cool and use for toilet facilities.

Instruct and show all clients the room they'll live in while on the project plus how things work, like the shower, microwave, refrigerator, where to get ice, coffee packets replenished and anything else pertinent to the use of the room, including hanging up clothes and the use of the iron and ironing board.

All rooms are to be non-smoking areas. Smoking is permitted in designated areas. Any client smoking in a room should be discharged from the program immediately.

It is suggested there be <u>no visitors</u> from the outside the project or any peer inside the program in the room of any client. Violation of this rule should result in dismissal from the program.

Room inspection by the counselors (with a security guard) is suggested to be random partly for cleanliness of the room and to assure there is no alcohol or illicit substances or non-prescription drugs in the room(s).

As a suggestion, should either alcohol or any illicit substances be found in a room at any inspection, the penalty should be immediate dismissal from the project.

The reason for using a motel room or its equivalent for a shelter for an individual in the project is that the room can be used as a workable training place for many of the lessons for cleanliness, hygiene, work, personal manners, as well as a counseling room when the room is used for training purposes.

Another reason for using a motel room instead of a general shelter with homeless and non-homeless people mixed in the shelter is that every night the homeless person has a safe consistent shelter.

When lodged in a city shelter, the homeless person may be in the shelter for a night or two and then on the streets the rest of the time. Being on the street disrupts the progress of the homeless person's transition from being homeless to ending homelessness.

For example, it is difficult to study in a city shelter or on the street, go to school for mechanic training in dirty clothes, not having a shower for several days, lacking sleep and food and so on.

Then too, the project homeless client in a motel is away from the street drug sellers or alcohol purveyors, the mind games and other distractions the street offers. Excluded also are the dangers of bullies, thieves, and other individuals who market harm.

The homeless he/she is in a protected, safe environment and continuing to progress toward ending homelessness.

Another reason of housing homeless persons in a motel or motel like environment is that there is privacy and quietness for the individual including separation from peers.

The decision of when to study, sleep or relax is the resident's of the room and more like the atmosphere he/she is likely to have in returning to the community and its society.

Then too, instead of putting every

thing one owns in a pack and carrying it around, clothes can be ironed and hung in a closet, the pack stored in the closet and when going out it isn't necessary to carry a pack.

Motel rooms are a convenient place for pick up by a bus or other vehicle to transport students to a GED or other classes. A client can board a bus to go shopping or elsewhere.

Bussing is particularly important when the clients are taken to a grocery store for a grocery purchase lesson arranged with the manager of the grocery store. Lessons may be more than one lesson, depending on the valuation of the grocery experiment by the Project Director.

The grocery store purchase lesson has a specific budget and the first lesson is to allow the client to purchase whatever is wished within the budget. Not one penny more is allowed to be spent.   It is interesting to note how cashiers and the store manager will cooperate with this lesson, once they know the purpose of the lesson or lessons.

Contact ahead with the manager pays great dividends in the lesson results.

The grocery budget lesson for each client is funded by the project, as are subsequent lessons if they are used. Use a specific amount such as $20...and not a penny more.

The first budget lesson is usually in the early evening after supper is served. When the client and his/her groceries are transported back to the motel and those items requiring refrigeration placed in the refrigerators.

Then the entire group is told that the next day no meals will be served, except supper. For the majority of the day, clients are to eat whatever edibles they bought on the grocery store budget purchases. There may be exceptions to this procedure, e.g., children involved, special diets, etc.

On the day following, meals will resume and grocery store purchases will be discussed with their counselors during the next day, as well as their respective case progresses.

It is strongly suggested also that counselors discuss with their clients the wisdom of food selections for a nutritious diet and why it is important.

Homeless people living on the street usually have little food selection capabilities, so before graduating from the project, they should learn what is recommended that they eat. They may require relearning of how to eat properly.

So, motel rooms or their equivalent have versatility and are useful for homeless men and women in a project to end homelessness.

For those locales who have sufficient housing and meals for homeless people, consider using the housing and meals similar in the same way as this motel concept and include in those homeless programs some of all of the suggestions.

Another suggestion is to budget for everyday clothes replacement to, with exceptions, eliminate the current clothing the enrollee is wearing plus clothes and footwear for daily use, employment, going to school and being in the public arena.

These should be new clothes purchased in such a way as to use combinations of clothing to a person's best advantage. The budget needs only to be adequate and appropriate for purchase in your locale. Some budgets are $200.00 for clothing.

Since a clothing budget is part of the project, a counselor's presence is required when the enrollee goes shopping for clothing selections, make suggestions and pay for the clothing.

Regarding meals, arrange with one or more restaurants to have meals served at certain times and places, unless a caterer or restaurant provides meal service and /or box lunches on occasion directly to the motel rooms by a certain time for each meal. Menus are approved by the Project Director. For excursions or other site travels, box lunches may be required.

Counselors need to regularly meet with clientele to discuss progress of the program in their clients' lives, what employment they'd like or may need to start with, if a person's ultimate goal isn't immediately available.

Also, most of the questions in CENSUS CHAPTER should be answered to make a more complete case study and include a counselor's comments too and any other helpful information.

Some clients may have been incarcerated in prison or jail or be on parole or just showing up in court.

If a counselor is willing, he/she might attend court with the client and talk with the judge about the program the client is enrolled in or could be enrolled in, then ask the judge to allow the client to continue or start the project to end homelessness rather than be sentenced.

Additionally whenever the client is to be in court, the counselor will be there as well to report the client's progress. Whenever possible, work with the Public Defender's office or other attorney, showing your program and what it can do for the client plus what benefits the client can have rather than what the usual sentencing results are.

It was my experience that many judges approved of the request to allow the client to be or continue in the project and report to the court at intervals as the judge stipulated regarding how the client was progressing.

At times an employer may be reluctant to hire a person who is discharged from prison or jail.

I encountered that philosophy on occasion.

I remember when I first encountered that barrier to work for a client. My answer to that employer was to ask if the employer would hire this person if a bond of $5,000 were available without cost to the employer or client to secure the employer from any loss due to the actions of the client?

The usual answer to me by the employer was, "Oh h_ _ _ , Herb forget the bond, just bring him/her in and we'll try the person out." As I understand that $5,000 bond is still available and can be found on the internet.

Every client should be examined by a physician with a counselor present to determine the status of the health of the patient and learn of any deficiencies which may prevent certain employment or other project activities.

Some clients may be eligible for Social Security and/or Medicare, Medicaid or Health Supplements.

The Project Director will need to decide if the project will, for the duration of the project, pay for a health care plan and/or supplement.

Clients who have or desire to fulfill their spiritual needs, as a suggestion, should be encouraged to strengthen that need because those who do usually appear to progress well.

However, the project rules will still need to apply because the project's purpose is to help the client return to the community and its society after which the client can pursue his/her spiritual needs as wished.

As early as possible and continuing throughout the project, it is important to determine the various deficiencies the client has and correct as many as possible which may hinder his/her progress, as well as find and encourage the positive assets available.

It is also important to learn and/or encourage the client's set goals to achieve while in the project.

Granted, the goals may be modified or change as the project continues, yet it is necessary to write them down on paper and review them daily, once in the morning on arising and once in the evening before retiring.

The reason for this is that when employment is sought, the kind of work the counselor knows the client is seeking makes it easier for the counselor to find employers who may be willing to train the client or may already have an employee training program which will fit the client.

Similar results can be obtained for certain education and other ideals.

Counselors can also prove to be excellent mentors, if they are interested to do so.

When the project includes a woman with a child or children, then the age of the child/children will determine the necessary services which need to be available to care for the child/children to help the lady terminate her homelessness.

Whatever the client is doing, the counselor needs to continually have contact with the client and review the resources the client is developing to use, so when the counselor can assist he/she will better able to do so.

In essence, the clients in a project of this nature are learning how to manage their lives effectively and discharge the clutter in their past lives.

These clients are also studying how to make healthy decisions which promote a positive life for them and those who will associate with them when they leave the project.

A project of this kind can be accomplished by an organization, government, business, individual or other entity. The program can be managed using sub-contracted services of other organizations or firms which will provide food management, shelter supervision and so forth.

Volunteers can be used efficiently and effectively to enhance project services plus learn to understand and assist the homeless person where necessary. The same concept can be used for new and present staff.

Funding will be required, as well as some publicity and perhaps some donations will surface.

Grantors when properly approached may be available for funding the homeless ending project. A Grantor may wish to know when their grant money is ended, how will the project continue?

A program of this nature requires goals and those goals will vary for each locale, as will the services provided to homeless persons.

As holidays occur, such as Christmas, Thanksgiving and New Years, in some way help those homeless people in the project celebrate the occasion, feel welcome and important during those days with a small gift, a dinner and/or a card...something in the project   to recognize that they belong to something while they are in this project/program.

For Christmas, for example, perhaps depending on the how their shelter is constructed, a Christmas tree or maybe two Christmas trees lighted, with ornaments and maybe tinsel could be seen from each window.

This will brighten most everyone's attitude and give hope which is something the homeless men, women and women with children need...desperately.

A Pilot Project may be the best way to begin to eliminate homelessness in your locale. It can give an opportunity to work out an excellent program design initially and address certain project aspects which weren't addressed in the planning phases in the initial project.

Length of the program may vary for each client because they have different experiences, education and willingness to work with the project. Every client very likely will progress differently and may leave the program at different times as they successfully return to the community and its society.

Before they leave, however they need to know:

- how to apply for work,
- refreshment in manners,
- ethics for their personal and business lives,
- how to talk with people,
- give a talk in front of an audience,
- how to give the best of their work to their employer,
- do the best in studies they take,
- keep their body healthy, and
- make friends.

When a client leaves the program, ask her/him when their finances are stable and the person is comfortable to help a homeless person in some way ...like buy them a meal or whatever the person wishes to do. In doing so, the project they came from will be repaid and if the person doing this will call in as to what they did (they need not identify themselves), the Project will appreciate this information.

As a suggestion, Project goals need to be well defined. The maximum length of the program needs to be determined.

Remember that as homeless people leave the program, use the waiting list to fill the vacancies.

Successfully exiting a project of this kind to end homelessness plus learning to handle the usual life problems will end the misery of homelessness which homeless persons have endured for so long.

The aforementioned suggestions for creating a program in your locale work because they've been used successfully in part and in whole and because the project you create specific for your locale is continuous to completion by providing the foregoing services mentioned. It provides consistent meals every day of the week and safe secure shelter which avoids street confrontations which can shatter a project's success.

As an additional note, when a Pilot program is initially constructed and designed to assist a specific number of homeless persons to rejoin the community and its society with employment and the homeless person's deficiencies corrected is usually of interest to several private and government entities using grant funding for the first one to three years.

Good records must be kept.

Governments such as cities, villages, townships and/or smaller entities can develop such programs in several ways. The concepts suggested in this treatise can be used and modified to fit your locale. Consult an attorney with your project/program design.

Regardless of the size of the entity which uses these ideas and suggestions to stop homelessness and end its misery, remember that if you sub-contract certain services set a reasonable goal of success of homeless rehabilitation and require documentation of the use of the funds given.

For example, state that a certain minimum number of homeless people must successfully exit the program by either with jobs or continuing academic education for entities providing those services and place a time limit for such a project.

Those entities which don't do the minimum required successes need a probation warning the first year and if the same failure occurs the second year, have a hearing with organization and if the explanation is unsatisfactory, then suspend the entity until it can prove its worthiness to be considered in the future.

Each year publish the contracts being sought to service the homeless program and request any firm, organization, non-profit, church, business or other entity or individual who wishes to submit a proposal, along with qualifications to deliver the service being contracted to do so. Then select the best proposals after an onsite visitation or whatever criteria is desired to be established for selection.

Regarding the various organizations which produce as much as they can in food, showers, laundry and other services, although they don't terminate the misery of a homeless person, still these services are helpful for the moment in time that these services are available.

Until complete projects providing food and nourishment plus safe secure shelters are available in such quantities to eliminate the need for such various organizations' random services, these well intended services should be encouraged.

The need for programs/projects to eliminate homelessness and its misery is great. It will take as many of us as want to help to design and implement such projects/programs to do so, as well as educate people in the greater populations to the need for such programs which is something, over time which you and I can do.

Reader...will you help your locale?

CERTIFICATE OF HONOR PRESENTED
TO **HERB ANDERSON**
BY THE CITY AND COUNTY OF
SAN FRANCISCO ON OCTOBER 17, 2008
WHEREAS, on behalf of the City and County of San Francisco, I am pleased to commend Herb Anderson for his outstanding and selfless service for years to the homeless people of San Francisco. Your unconditional dedication to changing the lives of those most in need in our community is befitting of our city's namesake. After ten years at Mission Hiring Hall it is my sincere honor to wish you all the best on your well deserved retirement. Best of luck on your future endeavors.
THEREFORE, I have hereunto set my hand and cause the Seal of the City and County of San Francisco to be affixed.

Gavin Newsom, Mayor
(Now Lieutenant Governor of California)

HONORS

CERTIFICATE OF APPRECIATION
TO **HERB ANDERSON**
In grateful recognition for years of philanthropic work
And service to the community the
Office of the Public Defender
Hereby Present

Herb Anderson

With this certificate of appreciation on your retirement

On this 17th day of October, 2008

Jeff Adachi, Public Defender
(City and County of San Francisco)

HONORS

HERB ANDERSON...
HAPPY RETIREMENT!

*Thank you for so generously
sharing your light and
inspiring us all.*

MISSION HIRING HALL
(City and County of San Francisco)

October 16, 2008

ABOUT THE AUTHOR

Herbert C. Anderson Jr., RPh, MS, FAACT, has a solid track record with more than sixty years of experience helping the homeless return to society.

His work earned him recognition by officials in San Francisco, California by honoring him for his results and accomplishments with the area's home-less people.

He recognized that the homeless person is one that has nowhere to go and...no hope plus most have in common that they lack guidance in how to stop being homeless and end its misery.

Working as a self-help copywriter and a consultant to homeless projects and programs, Anderson continues to make a difference through his efforts.

He can be contacted at:
herbandersoninfo@yahoo.com